WOMEN ARE HUMAN

WOMEN ARE HUMAN

TAMANA TAMANA JAN

Copyright © Tamana Tamana Jan
All Rights Reserved.

This book has been published with all efforts taken to make the material error-free after the consent of the author. However, the author and the publisher do not assume and hereby disclaim any liability to any party for any loss, damage, or disruption caused by errors or omissions, whether such errors or omissions result from negligence, accident, or any other cause.

While every effort has been made to avoid any mistake or omission, this publication is being sold on the condition and understanding that neither the author nor the publishers or printers would be liable in any manner to any person by reason of any mistake or omission in this publication or for any action taken or omitted to be taken or advice rendered or accepted on the basis of this work. For any defect in printing or binding the publishers will be liable only to replace the defective copy by another copy of this work then available.

- Acknowledgment

This book is about women right , mostly in doveloving countries and under developing countries they don t give any value for women right.

Women play a great role in the growth and development of the society and making it an advanced and modern society.

Without woman nothing is possible for men, they are basic unit of the society, they make a family, family make a home, home make a society and ultimately societies make a country. So the contribution of a woman is everywhere from taking birth and giving birth to a child to the care for whole life and other areas. All the roles and responsibilities of the women can never be neglected by the societies. Without education and women empowerment no development is possible in the family, society and country. Women know well how to talk, how to behave, how to deal with people of different classes, etc. She knows to handle all the situations because she knows well the basic fundamentals of a good society and play her roles politely as a main contributor in building a strong society.

Contents

Part 1

- Women are human!

A **woman** is an adult <u>femalehuman</u> Women are equally important in society as men are. They are the backbone for a progressing nation. Demographically, half a population of the country constitutes women, and they deserve equal importance and rights in society.

From keeping the home safe and clean to portraying excellent outcomes in the workplace, a woman can do it all. Their capabilities must not be underestimated based on their gender, and they should be given equal opportunity to display their talents. It is essential for us to know the status of women in our society, and therefore, we have compiled some extended, short, and ten lines essay on the role of women in society.

In the middle age, people had only one notion about the woman; that is, they were born to control the household chores and manage the children. But in today's world, women empowerment has taken place which has opened new doors for the women to thrive and shine.

In the rural regions, the girls have started going to school, which is positively affecting the literacy rate in India and is taking the country in the forward direction. Campaigns are held all over the country to spread awareness about woman literacy.

In addition to literacy, personal health and hygiene are other issues that woman staying in the rural region have very less idea about. Women hold awareness programs and free sanitary napkins are distributed amongst them. Such a programmed is organized to remove a general taboo about the menstrual cycle.

Besides managing household works, women are also engaging themselves in the service sector like banks, hospitals, airlines, schools and every other possible work field as well as they have started showing interest in setting up their own business. Not to mention, they are providing excellent outcomes in their respective areas. In the world of sports, women have set up milestones for men to achieve.

Personalities we must not limit or try to limit the role of women in society to be a homemaker or a mother because they are capable of doing so much more. The women who are homemakers are an essential member of the family who is responsible for managing the home, cooking, cleaning, and doing the dishes, taking care of the elders and the kids

Still, the saddest part is at times their efforts are overlooked, and they are never praised for the things they do. People assume these works as their duties and consider them to be a free servant. This outlook needs to change, and people should understand that she might even need some help in doing the works and she is not free labor, whatever she does is out of love and love only.

In the modern world, women are progressing. The social and economic status of the women have soared to height, and they are no longer confined within the boundaries of the four walls. They are playing the roles of a working woman, an efficient homemaker, and a proud mother and daughter.

Earlier women were only associated with taking care of the household and babies. But nowadays, they are engaging in work fields to explore their inner talents and also to become independent and earn for themselves.
They are one of the main reason behind the progress of the nation who makes our daily lives easy and the country proud.

To conclude, women should be encouraged to do something out of the household works, and if they already want to work in offices to earn for themselves, no one should stop them. They are an individual identity who have full freedom of doing anything that they think is the best for them.

- A woman should be given equal opportunities economically and socially.
- They must be respected and never underestimated on the ground that they are women.
- Schooling should be made available for the girls in the rural area.

- Awareness must be spread on the topic of sanitary health and hygiene.
- Their choice and perspective must be looked upon on as they are great leaders.
- During the middle ages, the women's position in the society became inferior as compared to men, and the condition of the women deteriorated.
- The women should be given freedom in whatever she does and should not be confined within four walls of the house.
- Women should be headstrong and believe in them. They must voice their option without any fear.
- People should start believing that motherhood is an option and the decision solely depends on a woman.
- We should remember the contribution of woman leaders and have a positive attitude towards woman controlling the government.

- Women rights are basic human rights claimed for women and girls all over the world. It was enshrined by the United Nations around 70 years ago for every human on the earth. It includes many things which range from equal pay to the right to education. The essay on women rights will take us through this in detail for a better understanding.

Importance of Women Rights

Women rights are very important for everyone all over the world. It does not just benefit her but every member of society. When women get equal rights, the world can progress together with everyone playing an essential role.

If there weren't any women rights, women wouldn't have been allowed to do something as basic as a vote. Further, it is a game-changer for those women who suffer from gender discrimination.

Women rights are important as it gives women the opportunity to get an education and earn in life. It makes them independent which is essential for every woman on earth. Thus, we must all make sure women rights are implemented everywhere.

All of us can participate in the fight for women rights. Even though the world has evolved and women have more freedom than before, we still have a long way to go. In other words, the fight is far from over.

First of all, it is essential to raise our voices. We must make some noise about the issues that women face on a daily basis. Spark up conversations through your social media or make people aware if they are misinformed.

Don't be a mute spectator to violence against women, take a stand. Further, a volunteer with women rights organizations to learn more about it. Moreover, it also allows you to contribute to change through it.

Similarly, indulge in research and event planning to make events a success. One can also start fundraisers to bring like-minded people together for a common cause. It is also important to attend marches and protests to show actual support.

History has been proof of the revolution which women's marches have brought about. Thus, public demonstrations are essential for demanding action for change and impacting the world on a large level.

Further, if you can, make sure to donate to women's movements and organizations. Many women of the world are deprived of basic funds, try donating to organizations that help in uplifting women and changing their future.

You can also shop smartly by making sure your money is going for a great cause. In other words, invest in companies which support women's right or which give equal pay to them. It can make a big difference to women all over the world.

To sum it up, only when women and girls get full access to their rights will they be able to enjoy a life of freedom. It includes everything from equal pay to land ownerships rights and more. Further, a country can only transform when its women get an equal say in everything and are treated equally.

It is essential to have equal rights as it guarantees people the means necessary for satisfying their basic needs, such as food, housing, and education. This allows them to take full advantage of all opportunities. Lastly, when we guarantee life, liberty, equality, and security, it protects people against abuse by those who are more powerful.

Women's rights are the essential human rights that the United Nations enshrined for every human being on the earth nearly 70 years ago. These rights include a lot of rights including the rights to live free from violence, slavery, and discrimination. In addition to the right to education, own property; vote and to earn a fair and equal wage.

Gender equality is not a 'women's issue' but affects both women and men, as it is rooted in the relationship between the two. Both women and men have to change their ways of working, attitudes and social norms, to ensure both are equal, empowered and dignified.

Rooted in the concept of equality within the family and community, we helped families to improve their food and income security. The focus on gender equality enabled women to form more equal relationships with men, and have greater control over their resources and assets, with equal participation and joint decision-making.

As you will see throughout this publication, the results of the program were significant and evidence the difference a gender equality approach can make, not only to individual lives but to whole communities.

Being a woman means **having a strong sense of identity**, accepting your body as one that adapts and changes over time, being confident, and building up the people in your life. It means you have the wisdom to be grateful for what you have while still being hungry enough for growth.

The woman performs the role of **wife, partner,** organizer, administrator, director, re-creator, disburser, economist, mother, disciplinarian, teacher, health officer, artist, Minister, prime minister and queen in the family at the same time. Apart from it, woman plays a key role in the socio-economic development of the society.

Main purpose of education is **to educate individuals within society**, to prepare and qualify them for work in economy as well as to integrate people into society and teach those values and morals of society.

Women's <u>empowerment</u> (or **female empowerment**) may be defined in several ways, including accepting women's viewpoints or making an effort to seek them, raising the status of women through education, awareness, literacy, and training. Women's empowerment equips and allows women to make life-determining decisions through the different problems in society.[3] They may have the opportunity to redefine <u>gender roles</u> or other such roles, which in turn may allow them more freedom to pursue desired goals.[1]

Women's empowerment has become a significant topic of discussion in development and economics. Economic empowerment allows women to control and benefit from resources, assets, and income. It also aids the ability to manage risk and improve women's well-being.[4] It can result in approaches to support trivialized genders in a particular political or social context.[5] While often interchangeably used, the more comprehensive concept of gender empowerment concerns people of any gender, stressing the distinction between biological and gender as a role. Women empowerment helps in boosting the status of women through literacy, education, training and awareness creation. Furthermore, women's empowerment refers to women's ability to make strategic life choices which had been previously denied them.

Nations, businesses, communities and groups may benefit from the implementation of programs and policies that adopt the notion of female empowerment. Empowerment of women enhances the quality and the quantity of human resources available for development. Empowerment is one of the main procedural concerns when addressing human rights and development.

There are several principles defining women's empowerment such as, for one to be empowered, they must come from a position of disempowerment. They must acquire empowerment themselves rather than have it given to them by an external party. Other studies have found that empowerment definitions entail people having the capability to make important decisions in their lives while also being able to act on them. Empowerment and disempowerment are relative to the other at a previous time; as such, empowerment is a process rather than a product.

Scholars have identified two forms of empowerment, economic empowerment and political empowerment. Rahman et al. said that empowering women "puts a strong emphasis on participation in political structures and formal decision-making and, in the economic sphere, on the ability to obtain an income that enables participation in economic decision-making.

Economic empowerment

Since the 1980s, the push for neoliberalism prioritizes competitiveness and self-reliance as a measurement for economic success. The individuals and their identifying communities that do not meet society's favored neoliberal standards are looked down upon and are prone to lower their own self esteem. Some groups who do not fit the preferable neoliberal image are the lower working class and the unemployed.

Specifically, neoliberalism has negatively impacted women's self-worth through its welfare reform policies. Mary Corcoran et al. theorize that conservative welfare reformers believe in welfare dependency as the cause of poverty. This leads welfare reformers to widen the criteria for an individual to qualify as a welfare recipient, limiting the number of people dependent on welfare. These criteria include: work requirements and time limits, rapidly pushing women into the labor market. The active push for women to enter the labor market reinforces the notion that single mothers and unpaid care laborers are unproductive to the American economy. In consequence, women are forced to settle for low-paying unstable jobs while having to manage their maternal and domestic responsibilities. Scholars believe welfare reform's underlying purpose is to disempower women by suppressing women's agency and economic independence. By creating opportunities for women empowerment like job training, women can counteract the social implications of neoliberalism and specifically welfare reform.

In addition, policy makers are suggested to support job training to aid in entrance in the formal markets. One recommendation is to provide more formal education opportunities for women that would allow for higher bargaining power in the home. They would have more access to higher wages outside the home; and as a result, make it easier for women to get a job in the market.

Women's empowerment and achieving gender equality helps society ensure the sustainable development of a country. Many world leaders and scholars have argued that sustainable development is impossible without gender equality and women's empowerment Sustainable development accepts environmental protection, social and economic development, including women's empowerment. In the context of women and development, empowerment must include more choices for women to make on their own.

Strengthening women's access to property inheritance and land rights is another method used to economically empower women. This would allow them better means of asset accumulation, capital, and bargaining power needed to address gender inequalities. Often, women in developing and underdeveloped countries are legally restricted from their land on the sole basis of gender. Having a right to their land gives women a sort of bargaining power that they would not normally have; they gain more opportunities for economic independence and formal financial institutions.

Race has an integral impact on women's empowerment in areas such as employment. Employment can help create empowerment for women. Many scholars suggest that when we discuss women's empowerment, discussing the different barriers that underprivileged women face, which makes it more difficult for them to obtain empowerment in society, is important when examining the impact of race in connection to employment. Significantly examining how opportunities are structured by gender, race, and class can transpire social change. Work opportunities and the work environment can create empowerment for women. Empowerment in the workplace can positively affect job satisfaction and performance, having equality in the workplace can greatly increase the sense of empowerment.

In the case women have the opportunity to settle for stable jobs, Women of color encounter a lack of equal accessibility and privileges in work settings. They are faced with more disadvantages in the work place. Patricia Parker argues that African American women's empowerment is their resistance to control, standing up for themselves and not conforming to societal norms and expectations. In connection to power, feminist perspectives look at empowerment as a form of resistance within systems of unequal power relations. Within the societal setting of race, gender, and class politics, African American women's empowerment in the work environment "can be seen as resistance to attempts to fix meanings of appropriate identity and behavior, where such meanings are interpreted as controlling, exploitative, and other- wise oppressive to African American women. When talking about women's empowerment, many scholars suggest examining the social injustices on women in everyday organizational life that are influenced by race, class, and gender.

Another methodology for women's economic empowerment also includes <u>microcredit</u>. Microfinance institutions aim to empower women in their community by giving them access to loans that have low interest rates without the requirement of collateral. More specifically, they (microfinance institutions) aim to give microcredit to women who want to be entrepreneurs. The success and efficiency of microcredit and microloans is controversial and constantly debated some critiques claim that microcredit alone doesn't guarantee women have control over the way the loan is used. Microfinance institutions don't address cultural barriers that allow men to still control household finances; as a result, microcredit may simply be transferred to the husband. Microcredit doesn't relieve women of household obligations, and even if women have credit, they don't have the time to be as active in the market as men.

Political empowerment

Political empowerment supports creating policies that would best support gender equality and agency for women in both the public and private spheres. Methods that have been suggested are to create affirmative action the global average of women who hold lower and single house parliament positions is 23.6 percent. Further recommendations have been to increase women's rights to <u>vote</u>, voice opinions, and the ability to run for office with a fair chance of being elected. Because women are typically associated with child care and domestic responsibilities in the home, they have less time dedicated to entering the labor market and running their business. Policies that increase their bargaining power in the household would include policies that account for cases of divorce, policies for better welfare for women, and policies that give women control over resources (such as property rights).[18] However, participation is not limited to the realm of politics. It can include participation in the household, in schools, and the ability to make choices for oneself. Some theorists believe that bargaining power and agency in the household must be achieved before one can move onto broader political participation.

Cultural Empowerment

As a progressive society, standing for women's rights and empowerment, we must stop viewing culture only as a barrier and an obstacle to women's rights. Culture is an integral and huge part of diversity and a medium that seeks to ensure women's equal opportunities it recognizes their freedom to take pride in their values, whether they are orthodox or modern in nature. This is not to say that centuries of abuse clothed in the spirit of culture should be allowed to continue, let alone be celebrated. Undoubtedly, traditions cloaked in the idea of empowerment should be objected to in light of feminism. For example, some research indicates that women only have an equal chance to have their written work published in peer-reviewed journals if the sex of the author is absolutely unknown to the reviewers.[32] This is a result of historical habitual culture which has led to lack of representation of women in literary and therefore, strongly demonstrated why all cultural legacies cannot and should not be celebrated or encouraged.

There is a need for equal cultural rights for women to be acknowledged and implemented which would in turn help to reconstruct gender in ways that would rise above women's inferiority and subordination. Furthermore, this would significantly improve the conditions for the full and equal enjoyment of their human rights on the whole as argued by the UN expert in the field of cultural rights, Farida Shaheed.

Shaheed continues to add that the perspective and contributions of women must transcend from the margins of cultural life to the center of the process that creates and shapes cultures around the globe today.[31] "Women must be recognized as, and supported to be, equal spokespersons vested with the authority to determine which of the community's traditions are to be respected, protected and transmitted to future generations.

In addition, feminists, specifically feminist organizers, focus on building relationships as a medium for creating women empowerment. Scholars claim that building relationships results in empowerment because the increasing presence of power gaps in society are due to the lack of relationships that are needed to bridge them. When it comes to forming and maintaining relationships, there needs to be a balance of both collaboration and conflict between the two parties. Conflict commonly arises in situations where community members attempt to build relationships with external power figures like government representatives. Fostering a space for collaboration as well as deliberation of conflicting ideas is important because sorting out disagreements[1] allows for the formation of trust between the parties In addition, conflict individually benefits the women participants because it fosters problem-solving skills[1] and opens them to a new pool of knowledge and perspectives on society. Scholars observe that building relationships has a depoliticizing tendency as the activity does not directly challenge the oppressive structures affecting women. A specific observation of this depoliticizing tendency is story telling. When building relationships, feminists encourage women participants to share their personal experiences involving gender oppression, rather than deliberate about strategies to approach the oppressive system.

Women empowerment can be measured through the Gender Empowerment Measure (GEM), which calculates women's participation in a given nation, both politically and economically. GEM is calculated by tracking "the share of seats in parliament held by women; of female legislators, senior officials and managers; and of female profession and technical workers; and the gender disparity in earned income, reflecting economic independence". It ranks countries given this information.

Some critiques of GEM is that it is not concerned with factors regarding society, such as gender, religion, cultural context, legal context, and violations of women's rights Gender empowerment measure attempts to make a consistent standardized approach to measure women's empowerment; in doing so, it has been critiqued that the account for variation in historical factors, female autonomy, gender segregation, and women's right to vote.

In which the United Nations Development Program measures the inequality between genders within a country. Some critique of this measurement is that, because calculations rely solely on the achievement distribution between males and females of a population, does not measure gender inequality; instead it measures absolute levels on income, education, and health[

A more qualitative form of assessing women's empowerment is to identify constraints to action. This allows for the identification of power relations between genders. Because this is a participatory process, it facilitates conversation on gender discrimination Comparing constraints on women at a later time also allows for any changes or expansion to be better identified. The evaluation of the development of women's agency allows for an evaluation of actions taken. These assessments must also be based on the action taken by women, and not external groups. External groups can help facilitate women's empowerment, but cannot bestow it on them.